MY GOVERNMENT
LOCAL GOVERNMENT

by Vincent Alexander

Ideas for Parents and Teachers

Pogo Books let children practice reading informational text while introducing them to nonfiction features such as headings, labels, sidebars, maps, and diagrams, as well as a table of contents, glossary, and index.

Carefully leveled text with a strong photo match offers early fluent readers the support they need to succeed.

Before Reading

- "Walk" through the book and point out the various nonfiction features. Ask the student what purpose each feature serves.
- Look at the glossary together. Read and discuss the words.

Read the Book

- Have the child read the book independently.
- Invite him or her to list questions that arise from reading.

After Reading

- Discuss the child's questions. Talk about how he or she might find answers to those questions.
- Prompt the child to think more. Ask: Do you know people who work in your local government? What issues are important to them?

Pogo Books are published by Jump!
5357 Penn Avenue South
Minneapolis, MN 55419
www.jumplibrary.com

Library of Congress Cataloging-in-Publication Data

Names: Alexander, Vincent, author.
Title: Local government / by Vincent Alexander.
Description: Minneapolis, MN : Jump!, Inc., 2018.
Series: My government | Includes index.
Audience: Age 7-10.
Identifiers: LCCN 2017056999 (print)
LCCN 2017055695 (ebook) | ISBN 9781624969393
(e-book) | ISBN 9781624969379 (hardcover : alk. paper)
ISBN 9781624969386 (pbk.)
Subjects: LCSH: Local government—United States—Juvenile literature.
Classification: LCC JS331 (print) | LCC JS331 .A495 2019
(ebook) | DDC 320.80973—dc23
LC record available at https://lccn.loc.gov/2017056999

Editor: Kristine Spanier
Book Designer: Leah Sanders

Photo Credits: Juanmonino/iStock, cover; svetikd/iStock, 1; REKINC1980/iStock, 3; sharpcharge/iStock, 4 (student); Science History Images/Alamy, 4 (painting), 5; Jim West/Alamy, 6-7; Taiga/Shutterstock, 8; 4nadia/iStock, 9; fstop123/iStock, 10-11; JamesBrey/iStock, 12-13; kali9/iStock, 14; AndreyKrav/iStock, 15; Monkey Business Images/Shutterstock, 16-17; Maica/iStock, 18-19; Steve Debenport/iStock, 20-21; James R. Martin/Shutterstock, 23.

Printed in the United States of America at Corporate Graphics in North Mankato, Minnesota.

TABLE OF CONTENTS

CHAPTER 1
How Local Governments Formed 4

CHAPTER 2
Different Governments 8

CHAPTER 3
Working Together 14

ACTIVITIES & TOOLS
Take Action! 22
Glossary 23
Index 24
To Learn More 24

CHAPTER 1

HOW LOCAL GOVERNMENTS FORMED

How was government formed in the United States? It started at the local level. The first **colonists** were ruled by Great Britain. But they **governed** themselves.

They held meetings. They **voted** on issues. They created rules to live by.

After **independence** from Great Britain, state governments were created. **Federal** government formed, too. This was the new **democracy**.

But towns and cities still needed local governments. Why? Local leaders knew the needs of their **citizens** best. And state leaders could not do all of the work. They had bigger issues to work on. This holds true today.

CHAPTER 2

DIFFERENT GOVERNMENTS

There are many different kinds of places to live. We can live in a city.

We can live in a small town.
Or we can live in the country.

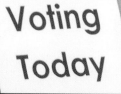

Leaders in different areas may have different names. County commissioners. Mayors. City council members. Township supervisors. City managers. They have one thing in common. They want us to have a better place to live.

Many leaders are **elected**. Who elects them? The people who live there.

TAKE A LOOK!

There are 89,476 local governments. They are in counties. Cities. Villages. Towns. Townships. Special districts. Some states have more than others.

Number of Local Governments per State

- ■ = over 3,000
- ■ = 1,501–3,000
- ■ = 751–1,500
- ■ = 750 and under

County government is the biggest form of local government. It provides services that are too costly for cities and towns. Like what? The sheriff's department. Airports. Jails. The roads between cities. Programs to help people who need **assistance**. Counties provide a court system. Counties might also offer libraries and parks.

WHAT DO YOU THINK?

Do you live in a city or town? What services does it offer? What services do you use?

CHAPTER 3

WORKING TOGETHER

What do citizens need from the local government? The services we use every day. Law enforcement. Fire departments.

Schools. Public transportation, such as buses and trains. Trash disposal and recycling.

How are services paid for? Citizens pay **taxes**. We pay them when we buy things. We pay them on money we earn. What is our biggest tax? Property tax. Anyone who owns property or land must pay taxes on it.

We also pay for **licenses**. A license gives you permission to own something. Or to do something. Like what? Drive. Camp. Fish. Even pets need licenses in some cities.

DID YOU KNOW?

Does your neighborhood have streetlights? Do you have clean water to drink? Local government provides these services.

Businesses pay for **permits** to operate. What kinds of businesses? All of them! Restaurants. Salons. Taxis.

Money from permits helps pay for services we use. Businesses must pay taxes as well.

Where else do **funds** come from? The federal and state governments. Often there is not enough money. Why not? Leaders do not want to raise taxes. Citizens can help. How? By volunteering. Donating to **charities**. We must all help to make our communities stronger.

WHAT DO YOU THINK?

Would you like to work in your local government someday?

ACTIVITIES & TOOLS

TAKE ACTION!

START A NEIGHBORHOOD ASSOCIATION

A neighborhood association is a group of people who want to make their neighborhood a better place to live.

❶ Does a neighborhood association exist already? Go to a meeting with an adult. Find out what they are working on. How can you help?

❷ If your neighborhood needs an association, hold a meeting of a small group of people. These could be homeowners, businesspeople, teachers, or others who live in your area. This small group can help you manage the larger association.

❸ Involve the greater neighborhood. Decide on a time and place to meet. Is there space in a park building nearby?

❹ Make a flyer to announce the meeting and distribute it to everyone in your neighborhood.

❺ Now hold your meeting. Let everyone discuss what they think the problems are in the neighborhood. Then discuss ideas for how to improve these problems.

❻ Decide when to meet next. At every meeting, discuss the progress members have made toward achieving the goals of the group. What more can be done?

GLOSSARY

assistance: Money that the government gives to people in need.

charities: Organizations that raise money to help people in need or another worthy cause.

citizens: Residents of a particular town or city.

colonists: People who left England to settle in America.

democracy: A form of government in which the people choose their leaders through elections.

elected: To have been chosen by a vote.

federal: The central power of the United States.

funds: Money provided for a special purpose.

governed: Made decisions about laws, taxes, social programs, and more in a certain area.

independence: Freedom from a controlling authority.

licenses: Official documents that grant permission for you to own, use, or do something.

permits: Official documents that give people permission to do certain activities.

taxes: Money that people and businesses must pay in order to support a government.

voted: To have cast a ballot, making a choice in an election.

CITY HALL

INDEX

businesses 18

charities 21

cities 6, 8, 10, 11, 13, 17

citizens 6, 14, 17, 21

colonists 4

county 10, 11, 13

court system 13

democracy 6

elected 10

federal government 6, 21

Great Britain 4, 6

independence 6

issues 5, 6

leaders 6, 10, 21

licenses 17

permits 18

services 13, 14, 17, 18

special districts 11

state governments 6, 21

taxes 17, 18, 21

towns 6, 9, 11, 13

township 10, 11

villages 11

voted 5

TO LEARN MORE

Learning more is as easy as 1, 2, 3.

1) Go to www.factsurfer.com

2) Enter "localgovernment" into the search box.

3) Click the "Surf" button to see a list of websites.

With factsurfer, finding more information is just a click away.